Let's read and talk about...

Healthy Eating

Honor Head

W
FRANKLIN WATTS
LONDON • SYDNEY

Franklin Watts
338 Euston Road, London NW1 3BH

Franklin Watts Australia
Level 17/207 Kent St, Sydney, NSW 2000

This edition © Franklin Watts 2014

Created by Taglines Creative Ltd: Jean Coppendale
and Honor Head
Author: Honor Head
Series designer: Hayley Cove
Editor: Jean Coppendale

Nutrition consultant: Sarah Bernard BSc (Hons), ARCS, MSc, RNutr www.eatwrite.co.uk
Series literacy consultant: Kate Ruttle is a freelance literacy consultant and Literacy
Co-ordinator, Special Needs Co-ordinator and Deputy Head at a primary school in Suffolk.

ISBN: 978 1 4451 3209 9
Dewey classification: 613.2
A CIP catalogue for this book is available from the British Library.

Picture credits
t=top b=bottom l=left r=right m=middle
Cover: front main pic AVAVA/Shutterstock; Julian Rovagnati/Shutterstock; back cover:
luchschen/Shutterstock
6 Benis Arapovic/Shutterstock; 7, Andrea Danti/Shutterstock; 8 Food Standards Agency;
9t Yuri Arcurs/Shutterstock; 9b Monkey Business Images/Shutterstock; 10 Julian Rovagnati/
Shutterstock; 11tl Richard Peterson/Shutterstock; 11m jerrysa/Shutterstock; 11tr Fotaw/
Shutterstock; 11b AVAVA/Shutterstock; 12t Andrew Olscher/Shutterstock; 12l Anna Sedneva/
Shutterstock; 12r Lepas/Shutterstock; 13 kristian sekulic/Shutterstock; 14 Varina and Jay
Patel/Shutterstock; 15l John Gough/Shutterstock; 15r Robyn Mackenzie/Shutterstock;
16 Teresa Kasprzycka/Shutterstock; 17t Monkey Buisness Images/Shutterstock; 17m Elena
Schweitzer/Shutterstock; 17b Ramzi Hachicho/Shutterstock; 18 Robyn Mackenzie/
Shutterstock; 19t Paul Cowan/Shutterstock; 19b Joe Gough/Shutterstock; 20l Natalia
D/Shutterstock; 20r Steve Lovegrove/Shutterstock; 21 Elena Elisseeva/Shutterstock; 22 Joe
Gough/Shutterstock; 23t glass Jeff Banke/oranges motorolka/carton Stephen
Coburn/Shutterstock; 23b Graca Victoria/Shutterstock; 24t luchschen/Shutterstock; 24b
Monkey Buisness Images/Shutterstock; 25 Olga Lyubkina/Shutterstock; 26 Monkey Business
Images/Shutterstock; 27t Robyn Mackenzie/Shutterstock; 27b Superstock; 28t
Hannahmariah/Shutterstock; 28b Graca Victoria/Shutterstock.

Printed in China

Franklin Watts is a division of Hachette Children's Books, an Hachette UK company.
www.hachette.co.uk

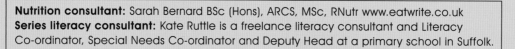

Contents

Pages marked with ⬇ have a free downloadable activity sheet at www.franklinwatts/downloads. Find out more on page 30.

Words in **bold** are in the glossary on page 29.

Why do I need to eat?

You need to eat to stay alive. Food gives you energy to move around. It also helps you to stay healthy.

How does food keep me healthy?

Food keeps you healthy because it contains nutrients such as **vitamins** and **minerals**. Nutrients help your body to grow, fight illnesses and to heal if you hurt yourself.

Food gives you the energy to play, enjoy sports and exercise.

TAKE ACTION

Write down everything you eat for a week. We'll come back to this on page 28.

Does a healthy diet help me to think better?

Yes, it does! Eating the right foods keeps your brain working well and helps you to learn. A good breakfast and lunch will also help you to stop feeling sleepy or moody during the day.

Why do I feel hungry?

When you feel hungry this is your body telling you it needs food to stock up on energy. Usually you feel hungry when your stomach is empty. But if you see a cake or smell your favourite food cooking, this can also make you feel like eating something.

Talk about

✪ **When do you feel hungry? Why do you think you feel hungry at these times?**

✪ **Do you swallow your food quickly or chew it a lot? Do you think it is better for you to chew your food well? Why?**

How do I get nutrients from my food?

1. When you chew, your food mixes with **saliva** in your mouth to become a mash.

2. When you swallow, this mash travels down a long tube called the **oesophagus**.

3. The mash then goes down to your stomach.

4. Next, it goes into your **intestines**.

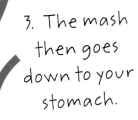

5. From your intestines, nutrients in the food pass into your bloodstream and travel around your body. Your body takes the nutrients that it needs. Everything else passes out of your body as **waste**.

What should I eat?

Fruit and vegetables

Starchy foods such as bread, rice, potatoes and pasta – these are called carbohydrates

To give your body all the nutrients it needs you should eat a balanced diet.

What foods make up a balanced diet?

There are four main food groups: **carbohydrates**, fruit and vegetables, **proteins** and **dairy**. Each group gives you some of the nutrients that are important to stay healthy. Try to include some foods from each group in your diet every day.

Meat, fish, eggs, beans and other protein foods

Milk and dairy foods

Does it matter when I eat?

Yes! It's important to eat breakfast because this gives your body energy after a long night of not eating. If you are always in a rush in the morning, aim to eat a slice of toast and peanut butter, or if you can't eat nuts try cereal with chopped fruit on top.

What about snacking?

Mid-morning and mid-afternoon snacks help to keep your energy levels up. Try to avoid sugary or fatty snacks such as sweets, biscuits and sausage rolls. Instead, try pieces of dried fruit, some low-fat cheese or fresh fruit or vegetables.

A good breakfast is a healthy start to the day.

Try some raw carrot sticks for a crunchy snack.

Talk about

✪ Do you eat the same sort of food all the time? Why do you think you like one food more than another?

✪ How do you think you would look and feel if you ate only one type of food for a week?

9

Why are fruit and vegetables good for me?

Fruit and vegetables help your body to work well and fight illnesses. You should aim to eat at least five portions a day.

Why five a day?

By eating five or more portions of fruit and vegetables a day you will get a good mix of nutrients to help protect you against illnesses, such as coughs and colds. You will also get plenty of **fibre** to keep your body in tip-top condition.

TAKE ACTION

Make a fruit salad using four fruits that you've never eaten before.

Eat different coloured fruits and vegetables for a mix of vitamins and minerals.

10

What is a portion?

A portion is an apple, pear or orange, three tablespoons of vegetables or one medium glass of fruit juice. For a rough guide, a portion is as much as you could fit in the palm of your hand.

Frozen, dried and tinned fruit and vegetables also count as part of your five a day.

Dried fruit

Frozen vegetables

Tinned fruit

Why is fibre important?

Fibre is important because it keeps you going to the loo regularly. Fruit and vegetables contain a lot of fibre. Eat the skin on fruit if you can as this has most of the fibre. Without fibre you could feel tired and you might not go to the loo properly.

Use fresh vegetables to make a salad.

Talk about

✪ What are your favourite fruit and vegetables, and your least favourite? Why? Is it taste, smell or the way the food looks?

✪ Do you think you eat enough fruit and vegetables? How do you think you could eat more?

How healthy are carbohydrates?

Carbohydrates are very healthy for you. They give you lots of energy for sports and games – and they are a good source of fibre.

How do I get carbohydrates?

You get carbohydrates from bread, rice, potatoes and pasta. These are healthy foods that give you lots of energy. You also get energy from fats, such as butter and cream, but these are not so healthy.

Why is brown bread best?

Bread is made from grains, such as wheat. These grains contain fibre. **Wholegrain** and brown breads contain more of the grain, so these breads have more fibre and are better for you.

Pasta

Rice

Brown bread

Potatoes

Try to get most of your carbohydrates from these foods.

12

Can I eat lots of carbohydrates?

That depends. The more you move around the more energy you use, so the more carbohydrates you can eat. If you eat a lot of carbohydrates and don't use them up by being active, your body will turn them into fat and this may make you overweight.

Lots of running and chasing use energy that you can get from carbohydrates.

Talk about

❂ **What sort of exercise do you do each day?**

❂ **How much food with carbohydrates do you eat each day? Do you think this is too much or too little for the amount of exercise you do?**

TAKE ACTION

Hold a bread tasting in class or at home. Try different types of bread such as bagels, pittas and chapattis. Read the packaging, if there is any, to find out which has the most fibre.

Read about Can I eat sweets and pies?

You should eat some foods from each of the four main food groups every day. Keep sweet and pastry foods as a treat.

What's wrong with sweet foods?

Most sweet foods such as chocolate, cakes and biscuits are made with sugar. Sugar contains lots of energy, but eating too much sugar can cause tooth decay. This means that you may need fillings when you visit the dentist. Many sweet foods also contain lots of fat. Fats and sugar can make you put on weight.

Which food do you think is better for you?

Sugary biscuits

Crisp fresh apple

14

Do I need fat for energy?

Yes, fats help to give you energy and some fats also help your body and brain to work properly. These good fats are found in nuts, seeds and oily fish, and vegetable oils such as olive oil.

TAKE ACTION

List your five favourite foods. How healthy do you think they are?

Talk about

✪ How do you think you would feel if you only ate sweets and pies?

✪ What fats do you eat that aren't very good for you? What food do you eat that has good fats?

Pork pie pastry is made with lots of fat.

Meat has a lot of fat.

These doughnuts are delicious but eating too many isn't good for your body.

Why are other fats not so good?

Pies, pastries, sausage rolls and cakes are made with fats such as **lard**, butter and margarine. If you eat a lot of these fats they can cause illnesses when you are older, such as heart disease.

15

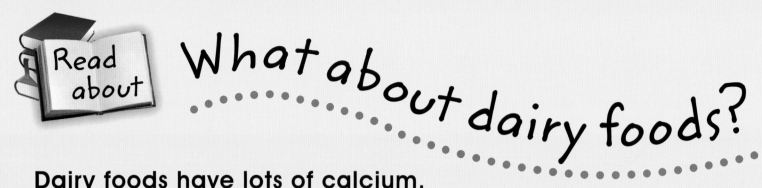

What about dairy foods?

Dairy foods have lots of calcium. Calcium is a mineral that builds strong teeth and bones and keeps your muscles working well.

What are dairy foods?

These are foods made from cow's milk, such as cheese, yogurt, cream and butter. Some dairy foods such as butter, cream and milk also contain fats. Too much of these fats can be bad for your body and they can make you put on weight.

Can I eat lots of dairy foods?

Low-fat versions of your favourite dairy foods are better for you. For example, if you like cheese, choose low-fat varieties such as Edam or cottage cheese. Keep cream and ice cream as a treat.

Cottage cheese on a roll with baby tomatoes and lettuce makes a tasty lunch.

Is milk a healthy drink?

Milk is packed with protein, calcium and vitamins, which you need to grow strong and healthy. Semi-skimmed milk is a great drink to have because it is better for your teeth than juices and fizzy drinks.

Can I get calcium from other foods?

Yes, you get calcium from leafy green vegetables such as cabbage, brown bread and **pulses** such as chickpeas.

Choose a glass of semi-skimmed milk instead of a fizzy drink.

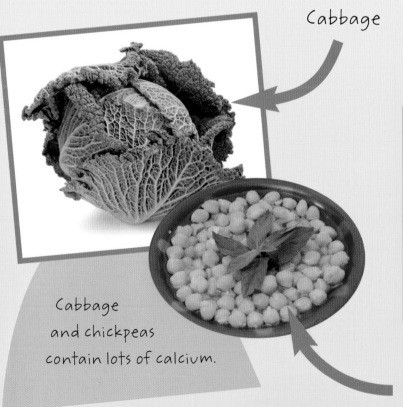

Cabbage

Cabbage and chickpeas contain lots of calcium.

Bowl of chickpeas

Talk about

✪ How much dairy food do you have a day? Do you think it's enough or too much?

✪ How could you include more calcium in your diet every day?

Why are meat and fish important?

Meat and fish are packed with protein. From your hair to your toenails, inside and out, your body needs protein.

What does protein do?

Protein helps your muscles, skin and body to grow and stay strong. It also helps your body to heal if you get a cut or a scratch. You get protein from foods such as meat and fish.

Lean meat such as turkey or chicken in a sandwich is a great way to get some protein.

TAKE ACTION

Burgers are packed with protein but try making your own. Use **lean meat** and grill them instead of frying.

Is all meat good?

Meat such as lamb and beef can be very fatty so don't eat too much. Keep ham, frankfurters and sausages as a treat. These meats also have a lot of fat, as well as added salt and **preservatives** to make them last longer in the shops.

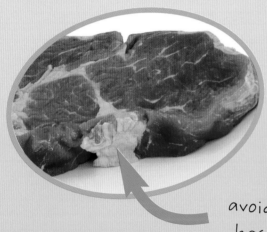

Try to avoid meat that has lots of fat.

Talk about

❂ Do you eat a lot of hamburgers? Why is eating too many ready-made hamburgers bad for you?

❂ How do you think you could eat more fish? What are some ways of eating fish that you could have in a lunchbox?

Which fish is best?

Choose oily fish such as salmon, tuna and mackerel. It is full of fats that help to keep your brain alert and your body in tip-top condition. White fish, such as pollock or plaice, is also very tasty.

Mix tuna with low-fat mayonnaise for a quick jacket potato filling.

Does it matter how food is cooked?

How your food is cooked changes how it tastes and how healthy it is for you.

Is fried food bad for me?

When food is fried it soaks up all the fat in which it is cooked, and too much fat is bad for you. Frying in vegetable oil or olive oil is a healthier choice than butter.

So what are the best ways to cook?

Try eating food that has been steamed, boiled or baked. Steaming is excellent because it keeps all the nutrients in the food. Stir-frying uses very little oil so it is also a healthy way to cook.

Home-made potato wedges baked in the oven are much better for you than fried chips.

Stir-fried chopped vegetables are quick to cook and good for you.

What raw food can you see on this plate?

Does food have to be cooked at all?

Well, you wouldn't want to eat raw potatoes, and uncooked meat can make you ill. But strips of raw green and red peppers, carrot sticks and pieces of cauliflower or broccoli are great with a dip.

TAKE ACTION

Do a survey to find out which way of cooking potatoes is the favourite – fried, baked, boiled or mashed. Is the winner a healthy option or not?

Talk about

✪ Do you think chips taste better than boiled potatoes? Why?

✪ What foods do you eat fried? How else could you cook them? Do you think they would taste better or worse?

What am I really eating?

Some pre-packed foods and ready meals may contain lots of additives. Some additives are not good for you.

What sort of things are added?

Preservatives are sometimes added to food to stop it from going bad so quickly. Flavourings, such as cheese and onion, are added to snacks such as crisps. Colourings are added to lots of different foods, from jams to curries, to make them look tasty.

How can I know what's been added?

Check out the list of ingredients. By law, all food suppliers have to list everything that they put into food. Also, read what's on the front of the packaging. For example, 'fruit-flavoured' may mean there is very little real fruit inside.

Choose baked beans that have reduced sugar and salt, and eat with brown bread.

A tin of baked beans may contain additives such as colouring, preservatives, sugar and salt.

TAKE ACTION

Collect some labels or boxes from packaged food. Look at the information on the packaging. Is it helpful or confusing? Do you understand it?

What else should I check out?

If tinned fruit is in syrup this may contain lots of sugar. Look for the words 'natural fruit juice' for a healthy choice. Choose tins of vegetables with less salt and sugar, and tuna in **spring water** rather than oil.

Read the label and choose sardines in tomato sauce rather than oil.

Most packaged foods have a list of ingredients and other information about what's inside.

Talk about

✪ Do you think some of the words on packaging are confusing? Why do you think that is?

✪ Are labels helpful or not? How could they be better?

What's best to drink?

Water! Your body is made up of mostly water. You lose a lot of water every day when you sweat and go to the loo.

Try mixing water with pure fruit juice for a refreshing and healthy drink.

Drink water to keep your brain and body working well.

What if I prefer fruit drinks?

That's fine, but you shouldn't drink too much fruit juice because it contains natural sugars and acids that can be bad for your teeth. Try mixing real fruit juice with water and only have it at mealtimes.

So, what am I drinking?

Pure fruit juice is full of vitamins but it could also have lots of sugar. Some fruit drinks don't have real fruit, such as **squashes, cordials** and fruit-tasting drinks. Shop-bought smoothies can be full of sugar.

TAKE ACTION

Next time you buy your favourite fruit drink, check the ingredients to see what's inside.

Mix fresh fruit with milk or yogurt and water to make your own smoothie.

Talk about

❂ **How much do you drink a day? Do you think it's enough?**

❂ **What's your favourite drink? Is it good for you and why?**

❂ **If a fruit drink is not made from real fruit, why do you think it might have a picture of real fruit on the carton?**

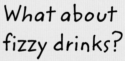

What about fizzy drinks?

Fizzy drinks are full of sugar. This can cause tooth decay and make you put on weight. One average-sized can of fizzy drink has as much as ten teaspoons of sugar in it.

What are the best snacks?

Snacks help to keep up your energy levels between meals. Choose the healthy options and leave the rest for treats.

What snacks aren't very healthy?
Avoid lots of crisps, sausage rolls, pies, sweets, chocolate and biscuits that are full of fats and sugars. Keep these as a treat for every now and again.

Try a bowl of raspberries and grapes for a healthy snack attack.

TAKE ACTION Make a school snack pack – each day fill a small plastic bag with chopped fruit, chopped vegetables or a seed and nut mix.

For a tasty lunchbox snack that's also good for you try chicken and salad wraps.

What's a healthy lunchbox snack?

The healthiest snacks are fresh fruit and vegetables, a small piece of cheese or a yogurt. Stock up with a bag of raw vegetable sticks such as carrots or green peppers to munch on.

What healthy foods can you see on this lunch tray?

Talk about

- ✪ Why do you eat snacks? Do you eat them because you're bored, tired or hungry, or because everyone else is?

- ✪ What are some healthy snacks you could eat?

What if I like crisps?

If you really want crisps pick unsalted ones and eat them with a tomato or salsa dip or some cottage cheese. Check out the packets for low-fat options or choose those with no **artificial** ingredients.

Talk about

☼ Check out your weekly food diary (see page 6). Did you have breakfast every day? Why is it important to have breakfast?

☼ Do you drink a lot of fizzy drinks? What healthy options could you replace them with?

☼ Why do you think peanut butter and banana on brown bread is a good choice for breakfast?

☼ What other fillings could you include in a pitta pocket?

☼ Are you eating lots of sweet and fatty snacks? If you are, what foods could you eat instead to improve your diet?

☼ Do you think that what you eat when you are at school can help your concentration or your mood?

Glossary

additives ingredients added to a particular food, such as colourings, that are not found naturally in that food

artificial something that is man-made

carbohydrates part of your food that gives you energy

cordials fruit syrups that you dilute (mix) with water to make a drink

dairy a food group that includes milk, cheese and yogurt

fibre the part of your food that helps your digestive system work properly and makes sure that you go to the loo regularly

intestines long tubes under your stomach where your food is broken down (digested and processed) so that your body can take all the nutrients it needs

lard a white, solid fat used for cooking

lean meat meat that has very little fat on it, such as skinned chicken

minerals substances found in some foods which help to keep our bodies healthy, for example calcium, which helps to strengthen bones and teeth

oesophagus the long tube that goes from your mouth to your stomach down which the food you have eaten travels

preservatives ingredients added to some foods so that they last much longer

proteins parts of the food that you eat which help you to grow muscles and keep you healthy

pulses seeds from plants that are used as food, such as beans and lentils

saliva also known as spit – the clear liquid produced in your mouth, which helps you to chew, swallow and digest the food that you eat

spring water water taken from a spring or river not from the tap, used in some tinned foods

squashes fruit drinks made from the flesh or juice of fruit mixed with sugar. You mix squash with water to make a drink

vitamins substances found in food that are essential to keep us healthy. There are many different vitamins, such as A and C

waste what is left from your food when it has been digested that comes out of your body as poo or wee

wholegrain the whole of the wheat grain

Index

Activity sheets

The following spreads have accompanying worksheets, which are available to download for free at www.franklinwatts.co.uk.

What should I eat? (pages 8–9)
Find out what is in your fridge and then fill in the blank food plate provided with drawings of the food you find.

Why are fruit and vegetables good for me? (pages 10–11)
Do a lunch box survey, fill in the tally chart and turn the information into a bar chart.

What am I really eating? (pages 22–23)
Fill in the sheet to find out which foods have the most additives.